String-Held Kites

String-Held Kites

Poems by

Lorraine Jeffery

Cover design by Shay Culligan
Cover image by Ali Karimiboroujenion on Unsplash
Tree image by Viktoriya Lissachenko on Unsplash
Author photo by Lorraine Jeffery

ISBN: 979-8-90146-799-2
Library of Congress Control Number: 2026941888

Kelsay Books
502 South 1040 East, A-119
American Fork, Utah 84003
Kelsaybooks.com

Acknowledgments

Thank you to the following publications, in which versions of these poems previously appeared in print or online:

Answering the Call (Oklahoma Anthology): "Adapting," "Childhood Forests"
Assignment Literary Journal: "Deep Valleys"
Best of Utah (League of Utah Writers): "Hearing Loss"
Book of the Year (Texas Anthology): "Fortification," "Bottled Ache"
Cadence (Florida Anthology): "A White Word," "Heartwood and Owls"
Calliope: "An Aria"
Clarion: "Homeplace"
Encore (National Federation of State Poetry Societies): "My Inheritance," "Stroke," "Grandpa's Barn"
Ensign Magazine: "Hands Across the Altar"
Ink to Paper (Indiana Poetry Society): "Night Watch"
Muleskinner: "Beginning Dust"
Ohio Poetry Days: "Two Gardens"
Parcham: "In the Beginning . . ."
Pennsylvania Prize Poems: "To a Husband"
Please See Me: "Cables and Carabiners"
Poetry (Pennsylvania Poetry): "Precious"
Sandcutters (Arizona Poetry): "Do You See Me?"
Sharing Nectar (Keysner Poets' Press): "If We Had Fashioned Each Other"
She Said Anthology (Utah Arts Council): "*Were You Angry?*"
Still Points Art: "I am from . . ."
Synkronicity: "Reunion Creek"
Vita Brevis Press: "For Myself"

Contents

I

Homeplace 15
I am from . . . 17
Deep Valleys 19
My Inheritance 21
Polaroid Pictures 22
In the Beginning . . . 23
Do You? 25
A white word 27
Grandpa's Old Barn 28
My Quiet Grandmother 30

II

Childhood Forests 35
Family Ties 36
Heartwood and Owls 38
Finding Your Way Home 40
On Purpose 42
An Aria 44

III

Rockfall 49
To a Husband 51

Divorce 52
If We Had Fashioned Each Other 53
Fortification 54
Adapting 56

IV

Bottled Ache 59
Question 60
Night Watch 61
Lost Son 63
So Little 64
Touch 66
Son with Schizophrenia 68
The Line 70
Two Gardens 72
For Myself 74
Reunion Creek 76

V

Beginning Dust 81
Were You Angry? 83
Cables and Carabiners 85
The Diagnosis 87
Stroke 89

Hearing Loss 90
I Miss You 91
Dementia 92
Precious 93
Bloodline 95

I

Homeplace

Wearing gratitude's shoes,
I come where parents taught
and siblings tattled.

Time spreads like ink
in a saucer of milk
set out for barn cats.

I see that the silo
is not so tall.
The house smaller
shabbier.

A loose screen door
bangs a resentful beat
while spiders concoct
their webby conclusions
and words play hide and seek
in the worm-eaten barnwood.

The garden has gone wild
reclaimed by the milkweed
we fought.
Pods spill white fluff—
tempting monarchs.

It was here that soil
soaked into my veins
as carefree hours stretched.

But bare feet are eventually
washed and shod.

Still,
I have learned how to shape
a window wider than a
door’s goodbye.
And I remember
every sigh the tombstones
have forgotten.

I am from . . .

After George Ella Lyon

rain and mud
brooms and shovels.
I'm from the rumble of
freight trains outside my window.
I am from grass, tall trees
and gladiolas.
From the huge maple tree that engulfed
the white two-story house.

I am from ocean beaches
cornmeal mush and family debates.
From loggers and nurses.
I'm from sleeping late
church on Sundays
and strong opinions on everything

I am from *use your head*
oh, my aching back
and big band music.
I'm from green Cascades
and trips to the Coast.
From homemade whole wheat bread
and store-bought potato chips.

I am from Reid and Eleanor's branch.
From aunts
on their way to dances
who changed their
mud-caked boots

for strappy high heels before
climbing into the old Ford.
From uncles who avoided fines on
overweight logging trucks.

I'm from black and white photos
which divide my childhood
into rectangles of time
rooted in tall trees and
salt water.

Deep Valleys

Tell me, I say to her ninety years.
Her smile fades as she remembers
her volcanic mother, and Della,
her stable oldest sister.

When things boiled up,
Muma threatened to drive
off Rocky Point
and kill herself.

I couldn't stay overnight—
ever.
She might be gone
when I got back home.

I don't know why,
she erupted at Della.
Muma was sewing and she
grabbed the scissors,
held them up like a knife,
over her chest,
said she was going to kill herself.

Della yelled something,
and Muma hesitated.
Hot tears ran down my face,
I couldn't move.

Then Della tackled her,
they went down yelling,
and Della grabbed the scissors.

When it was over,
I couldn't talk—
for three days.

She shrugs and smiles again.
It was so long ago,
but silent tears run down
the deep valleys
of her cheeks.

My Inheritance

My child fingers stroked her blue-veined hands.
        Thin skin pulls away
        from feather fragile bones.

I pulled and released.
        Tiny wrinkles disappear
        and reappear.

Spotted with sprinkled
        chocolate.
Scarred from paring knives,
        broken glass.

Ring finger permanently indented,
        ridged nails,
        no manicure.

She is gone,
        but her hands
        rest in my lap.

Polaroid Pictures

A Terza Rima

I view these pasted pictures with a sigh,
when relatives were still strong and young.
Memories take me back to days gone by.

That generation's songs have all been sung.
They stood in bobby socks, dresses and suits.
Aunts had shapely curves and skirts that clung.

Uncles had trousers, hats and working boots.
Then they had that famous reunion fight
and I first observed shaky family roots.

Each one knew that he or she was right.
It was '61, I think—September.
They all got over it—no time for spite.

Now all my months have become December.
I'll revisit—till I don't remember.

In the Beginning . . .

Childhood was tall trees
and grassy fields. At five,
I was the oldest, my brother,
still a baby.

And then there was my foster
brother, Mark,
four years older,
who crowded my top position—
just a bit.

***

Mama's "dejunking." Holds up a
battered rubber *drink and wet
doll*—one arm missing.

Do you want this? she asks me.
I shake my head and return
to coloring.

I do, Mark says suddenly. *I want
the rubber tube that's inside, I'm
going to make something.*

And the snake rears his ugly head.
I changed my mind,
I cut in, *I want it.*

Mama looks at me and must see
the flick of the forked tongue.
Mark asked for it first,
she says, handing it to him,

and evil is born.
I know why I want it—
because he does.

Do You?

I know you love me,
        I hear it every day.
        Mommy loves you,
        that's what you say.

But do you see me?
        Do I look different from the others kids
at school, from Joey or Clair?
        I don't wear glasses like Brian,
but he says we have the same hair.
Do I think the same thoughts
as Kevin or Shay?
Am I different inside or
am I okay?

        Am I the kind of kid you planned?
        What do you want me to be?
        When Mrs. Shaw said I was *out-of-hand,*
        you looked at her, not me.

        Did you see me?

She says we are all different.
        Did you know that Mom?
        Am I different in a good or
bad way—or is she wrong?

I know you love me,
          but
do you
see me?

A white word

on the red sign,
four letters—
ssssss, tt, oh or *o,*
pp. Ssstop!

Our car has to stop.
Not just because of the
red sign but because
of the white marks.

I hear the hum of our car
but I'm far away,
thinking about the curvy
lines that form letters.

My eyes search for words
on store fronts
but we're moving
too fast for me to sound
them out.

Still,
now I know that
the books at school
can tell more
than stories.

That black letters
will mark my world
forever.

Grandpa's Old Barn

There's nothing there, says Grandpa,
but I know it isn't true.
His barn's like a museum,
and there's lots of things to do.

I pretend-drive the green tractor,
while sitting on the metal seat
and I watch the tabby cat
slink by on padded feet.

There's some big machines, bales of hay,
dusty saddles and rusty pails,
ropes, chains and boxes of screws
and wire, old pipes and bent nails.

Once, I found a nest of baby mice—
wrinkled pink in the morning light.
They were squirmy and had no hair
and their eyes were scrunched up tight.

There's a special place where ants
climb up the scratchy wall,
and today, I heard a black beetle,
clicking away in the old horse stall.

Once, when I was sitting quiet,
        you won't believe what I saw.
A big brown snake with stripes,
        slithering out of the straw.

The barn smells like long ago,
        of cows, horses, hay and dust,
of oil, wood, straw and leather
        and old machines that rust.

The pigeons in the hay loft coo
        and fly as close as they dare.
While I explore the barn again.
        There's so much there.

My Quiet Grandmother

They were one—
the kitchen, my grandmother
and the black wood stove.
A kitchen thick with browning butter
and silence.

No opinions in an
opinionated family.
No anger, no hateful stares
no scathing words
but—
no spontaneous laughter

Her eyes smiled at children
and grandchildren
and she lied once about who broke
the door on the black oven.
"I did it," she said to
protect her young daughter
from his wrath.

This woman of work—
who was she?
Why so parsimonious
with her smiles and laughter?

Did she have her own
hopes and dreams?
Did she reheat the remains
of her wishes on
the stove of her soul?

My grandmother, the stove
and the kitchen.
She died at fifty one.
Was her life left lingering
in the ashes?

II

Childhood Forests

A minute

Douglas fir, pines, maple, hemlock—
memory's bedrock.
Limbs protected
and connected.

Never threatening, brooding, dark,
while sappy bark
needles and cones
formed earthly bones.

Mine was a safeguarded childhood.
All that was good
comes with the breeze—
memory's trees.

Family Ties

Were the ends of
the sibling ropes
already frayed?

I don't remember
what I said
when we were
discussing
Dad's care.

I was so mired
in my own muck,
that I responded
without thinking
and you lashed back—
severing our knot.

And all these years,
you have said nothing.
Letting your fury
fester in silence?

Or could you be like me,
feeling a dull ache,
like where a tooth
used to be.
Trying to untangle
how to break the
silence of a
never-ending
lament.

Heartwood and Owls

My people were Northwest loggers. I knew
pond monkeys, chokers, and gyppos. On
the playground, I breathed the paper mill stink
of Weyerhaeuser and Georgia-Pacific,
          like everyone else,
          scanned the green hills
on the lookout for a flash of flame,
when the fire risk was high and the woods
were closed.

After Long Tom, Seneca, and Pendleton mills
shut down, with ten-year-old eyes,
I saw the slash cuts, gashes,
discarded branches, logs, needles
and wood debris lying
every which way.

I heard the loggers curse *tree huggers* and
saw the bumper stickers,
I love spotted owls . . . fried, when
          unemployment hit
          twenty-five percent
          in lumber towns.

We have to save our forests,
the long hairs chanted.
          We fought and made up.

Fifty years later, I return. Weyerhaeuser
is farming trees, reseeding slash cuts,
filling gashes, reseeding
after Mount St. Helens
blew every which way.

Finding Your Way Home

You got out early.
I could say, *ran.*

I knew
you would come
to stand beside me.
The smoke of him
visible in your
gene-mimicked smile.

Dad drank the threads
of his paychecks,
while weaving our
sibling tapestry.

He loaded
his children' pockets
with the living
and the dead.

Now, he brings us
together like rain falling
into the same lake
it rose from.

I see him
in your walk
your gestures.
You have his eyebrows.

On Purpose

I stalked
my shy, quiet father.
I was almost fifteen
before I realized he
blushed and squirmed when I
gave him a hug.

Not a physically demonstrative man,
he hugged my mother.
But not often and even then
oh, so awkwardly.
He cuddled with babies but as
my siblings and I grew older—
he backed off.

As a teenager I grinned wickedly
as my perverse nature surfaced.
I purposely went out of my way
to hug him and feel his
shoulders hunch.

He knew he wasn't supposed to reject
his daughter or try to distance himself.
He had read the psychology books but
he wasn't comfortable with hugs—
forget kisses.

When cancer was slowly eating him
I came with my children
to say goodbye.

As we left
I tortured him one last time
hugged his emaciated body
and held on tight.
This time
he didn't squirm.

An Aria

How did sheer joy come
through eight hundred miles
of phone line?
Somehow, it did.

It's not like my brother is a
whining Eeyore.
He's a regular guy,
doing what must be done.
Taking care of a disabled
son, helping his wife,
remodeling the house,
paying bills.

But today,
today he telephoned and
delight flowed down the line.
Somehow, I knew his smile
was wide and his breathing deep.

He had allowed himself
a weekend alone—chosen a
three-day opera in a different city.

The Germanic Wagner? Really?
Ours wasn't a house of arias.
Growing up, we didn't even know
who Wagner was.

But I hear the ring of my brother's
voice in his ride of the Valkyries
away from responsibilities.
An unburdened respite—
of joy.

III

Rockfall

I'd carved my petroglyph
hopes in bedrock.
Saturday mornings with children
calling from rubble-filled
bedrooms, long conversations
after wiping coffee grounds
off granite counters.

Gone now
in a stony silence.
A wagon full of questions
pulled by blinkered draft horses.

Walking lighter now,
without the pebble in my shoe.
I stride to the office,
sometimes looking
for cell phone messages
I know won't be there.

Tonight, I'll be in a new
restaurant, straining to
move boulders with
friends and laughter.

I'll go on that European trip,
the one *we* talked about,
to see Gothic arches and
marble statues. I won't

have to compromise,
can be self-determining,
do what I want.

No need to look back
and turn to stone.

To a Husband

Yesterday, I was truthful,
not brutal or accusing—
        just candid.
It was a small thing.

You were silent,
but your disapproval
        surged through the house,
        warped the floors
        and dripped down
        the walls.

Divorce

The house
shatters
from
an earthquake
of deceit,
a splinter of Mom cries,
a shard
of Dad scowls.

The cement
foundation
cracks,
rebar bends,
a shred
of Sofie shouts,
a fragment
of Foster glares.

Roof joists shift,
a wedge of wall
splits.
The house
fractures,
staggers,
collapses—
the essence
of family
dies.

If We Had Fashioned Each Other

A Sonnet

If you had been designer Calvin Klein
and I had been a real Coco Chanel,
you'd have been taller, at least five foot nine,
I would have been more sexy—a bombshell.

I would have been softer, less defiant.
You would have liked traveling more, gardening less.
I'd love to cook and be more compliant.
Would we have failed as designers? Oh, yes!

We might have forgotten, *undemanding.*
Tenacity wouldn't have made the list.
We wouldn't have written *understanding*
and your handyman skills would've missed.

But we came readymade, were bought off rack
and neither would take the other one back.

Fortification

Our progress was slow
as we hefted the heavy
gray stones
of actions, words,
and apologies,
stacking them on one
another—
reaching
for the sky.

We mortared the stones
with love and shared
experience. We
stood side by side
with swords unsheathed
defending
the protective moat
with the drawbridge
of choice.

We built lookout turrets
and arrow slits
in case of attack.

While building
the bulwark,
we wove our
separate threads
together,
creating a coat-of-arms—

our identity
hanging in the
castle's great room.

Adapting

A Sonnet

So many years have flown like string-held kites
and angry words have slid down canning jars
as we have pulled together through long nights
of sick kids, paying bills and fixing cars.

But still, sometimes your actions drive me nuts
and there are times I'm sure you feel the same.
Still, we are who we are, no ands or buts,
no alterations here, it's how we came.

We've often moved, with houses bought and sold.
Lived through crisis, love, laughter, grief and tears.
We're past the paper, wood and now we're gold.
Flawed people stayed together fifty years.

Now that we're old enough for Medicaid—
it's obvious that we came readymade.

IV

Bottled Ache

I pack the peaches into jars
cover them with boiling syrup
submerge them in a
water bath.
I'm preserving them.
Making them stay.
For months?
Years?

I couldn't make her stay.
The clinic called it blighted ovum.
I called it Elizabeth Ann.
The pain is preserved
processed.

Peaches press
against the glass
aching to get out
but I stack them
on the shelf like
straight-lined soldiers—
saving them.

Question

A Nonet

As I soothed the baby, she surveyed
the messy kitchen and littered
living room. She planted her
little legs and then, hands
on hips, eyed me and
asked her question.
Is being
a mom
fun?

Night Watch

About curfew . . . he had nodded his young head,
Sure, sure. No Problem. That's what he said,
before his cell phone broke.

1:00 a.m.
Awake
Blankets thrown back.
Late. Beetles hitting lighted windows.
He'll be here soon

1:05 a.m.
Sirens screech
north. *He should come from the south.*
Lighted clock ticks

1:10 a.m.
Quick breaths
Watch car lights, picture skidding
brakes locked on icy roads.
Just late

1:15 a.m.
Pacing
Floor creaks under bare feet,
I see a car crumpled, blood,
siren cut short.
Next lights will be his

1:20 a.m.
Heart racing

Visualize headlights filtering through
water, hands groping for seat belt
release. *Breathe,*
he's just late

1:25 a.m.
Late!
Late!
Blood and sirens
late!

Car lights,
door opens.
He's home
and sees
only anger.

Lost Son

I cannot weep.
        The tears would overflow
        the banks of my soul
        and drown me.

I fear the god you worship,
        the needle to Nirvana.

I dread the call
        that will come one black night.
        Your god will extract further sacrifice—
        you or someone else.

How can I pray for
        a cell's cold rock walls,
        a razor wire fence?
        How can I?
        But I do,
        I do.

So Little

A Villanelle

You took a different path, another way.
We offered choices, but you decided.
Was there so little we could do or say?

We loved and taught you every single day
but your decisions were all short-sighted.
You took a different path, another way.

Our influence waned and your friends gained sway,
you rejected what we had provided.
Was there so little we could do or say?

Broken rules, then laws you wouldn't obey.
We sought others' help and were united.
You took a different path, another way.

Prison, lost years, consequences today;
your son gone and relationships blighted.
Was there so little we could do or say?

Now you're older and would like to replay.
If we could grant that, we'd be delighted.
You took a different path, another way.
Was there so little we could do or say?

Touch

A shy man,
my father only hugged us
when we were very young,

Unknowingly,
as a parent,
I reflected him;
cuddling my children
when they were small
but with the older ones
it was the arm around
the shoulder, a smile
that said, *I love you.*

And then
the isolation began.
We said words
did elbow taps
smiled, waved
kept a distance.

Who knew I would long
for human touch—
skin against skin,
to feel safe
in an embrace?

Would even miss
the warm handshake
of a stranger.

When loved ones returned
my arms enveloped them
and held on—
not shy.

Son with Schizophrenia

My son never declared himself lost
he just disappeared
into the city concrete
swallowed by a street
cratered by a curb
stamped out by a sidewalk.

I don't know what the backpack
of rejection weighed
but it must have been heavy
with failed hopes.
An orphanage
two failed adoptions
a world of cross-armed faces.

He found hope once
tried to hang on
but she disappeared
in an ambulance.
Abandoned again
he was haunted
by thoughts as
unsettling as reality.

He tried to fill the hole
in his soul
with pills
and illusions.

My grief never
declared itself lost.
My backpack
reality-heavy.

The Line

Of course
I'd seen the problem
on the
nightly news—
heads-down people,
tents, trash,
city officials with
no answers.

But today
on public transport
en route to a
restaurant
we round a curve
and I see them.

Like pictures of the
bread lines in
The Great Depression—
dark clothes,
slumped shoulders
standing patiently.

I sit in my restaurant
of choice, eat
tasteless food
and think of my
forty-year-old son
who is sometimes
homeless.
Is he in line?

Two Gardens

My age-spotted hands, still turn catalog
pages. I note the projected height, and
color of tulips, lilies, roses; check
productivity of beans, peas and squash.
.

Much easier than my human garden,
where some of my children were
transplanted from other soil. But even
those from my own seed packet,
yield unexpected results.

While cultivating both gardens,
I chastised myself for overwatering or
underwatering, for planting
too close, too shallowly, too deeply;
for weeding too much or
not enough.

Experts differed on proper care.
Always looking over the fence,
I watched my neighbors water
and weed, worried that they were
better, wiser gardeners than I.

This winter, my yard garden has gone,
my children—grown and become.
Flowers all, but not the closely weeded
beds and sharply trimmed hedges
of English gardens.

I value my well managed outside garden,
but I am awed by my unorganized,
unpredictable human garden,
flowering on its own,
bursting with energy in
turbulent waterfalls of
dazzling diversity.

For Myself

Heavenly peace words,
cradled in my mother's hands had
comforted, but now my own small
children stare as tears stream.
In coming years, I will water
thirsty eyes with many more
torrents—but this is my first loss.

Oldest grandchild on both sides,
my aunts' new dresses draped
slim figures, my uncles
flexed strong muscles, while
agile grandparents gathered us.

This was my huggable
nurse-grandmother who owned
a care center, lived by the lake,
and wore the red and black
coat I called her chili bean coat.

She who had stood in the doorway
of the bathroom, as I applied
my teenage blue eye shadow,
and stated flatly, *I've seen
dead people who had blue around
their eyes like that.*

But I'm a mother now. After a phone call,
I can't just quit cooking lunch,
retreat behind a closed bedroom door

and curl around the hole in my heart,
but I do.

My Christian husband, tries to comfort me,
She's all right where she is.
I stare at him and say,
She's not the one I'm crying for.

Reunion Creek

The creek was bigger,
when chilly water
    tickled my toes
        and my small feet
    slipped on slick rocks.
I shivered in my muddied clothes,
while Mom wrapped me in an old quilt,
for the long ride home.

Later, when my mind
was filled with algebra, and I read
the future in tee shirts and jeans,
I left the younger cousins,
walked up the creek and
gathered the quiet, like moss gathers
life-giving water.

Later still,
I loaded my children into the van
and they arrived amid squeals of delight.
My time to scrape mud from shoes,
bring potato salad and
towels to cocoon wet children
for the ride home.

Now I sit,
chasing shade, listening to the creek's
murmur. My arthritic knees would
struggle going down the steep bank,
but I could do it.

Could feel the water's cool
brush strokes once again,
hear the susurrus of leaves.
But there is no one to quilt-wrap me
for the long ride home.

V

Beginning Dust

This tech generation of
grandchildren, arrive
with phones, videos,
apps and games, to ride
4-wheelers down dusty trails.

No sparkling stream—
this is drought country,
and dust coats the rental
cabin when ATVs grind by.

Nearby dead undergrowth
has been cleared around
tree trunks, branches hacked
off at various lengths,

Bored children troop outside.
Thump!
I listen and wonder.
Click, thud. thump,
snap, clickety, click
bang,   clack.
Click, thud. Thump!

I go to the back door—
three kids, hands clutching
assorted sticks, hit trunks,
sawed off branches,
tapping, cracking,

thumping out a
syncopated rhythm.

They sway and step
in counter point,
each jazz player listening
to the others and adding.

Thump, whack, click.
Ancient DNA dancing
back to stones and sticks;
they once again
create beginning music.

Were You Angry?

With grandmotherly wisdom,
I explained that university doors
have opened much wider since
my college days.

I had been expected to major
in nursing or education. Either one
would have allowed me to supplement
my husband's real job.

Were you angry about that?
my granddaughter asks
stirring her drink
with a paper straw.

I pause a minute
before answering the question
I had never considered.

No,
I finally say. *I compared*
my opportunities with those of
my mother and grandmothers.
College was not possible
for them.

Only much later, do I think of my
father and grandfathers who,

finances permitting, could have
and did attend college.

I had instinctively looked for
role models on my maternal side.
Can I open the door
a bit wider for
those women who follow me?

Cables and Carabiners

Holiday card displays,
in leotard colors
of magenta and glittered gold
convey messages—
tender, amused, caustic.

Twin holidays—
Mother's Day ascends ladder
rungs to Father's Day.

For years, I bounced babies
in front of these racks,
pondering, considering,
selecting mine and making sure
the much-loved son
didn't miss the trapeze swing.

Choosing the exact card
to match my mother's smile or
his father's grin. Trying
to anticipate misty-eyes or
belly laughs.

Now, my chalked hands grip
a bar and I stand
on arthritic feet
conscious no address
will deliver
a loved one.
I swing above the abyss,
knowing
there is no safety net.

The Diagnosis

Dad's cancer rooted like crab grass
and s p r e a d

I
was young
dreaming beyond my fingertips

The future beckoned while
walking on ice through his storm
of medication and appointments

He
could deal with the illness
but not the loss of usefulness

His mouth was sharp and demanding
when despair's booted foot
pressed on his neck

We
lost the dictionary
and lived under steelwool skies

Silence in oneself is hardest to forgive

I
conceal my regret
behind his shadow

Bowing down
for thirty years
on bloodied
knees

Stroke

A Haibun

My fighter pilot limps home on one wing. Lands in a heap but he climbs out—kind of. He doesn't remember the day we met. Knows me, but not how to put on his shoes. Repairmen swarm—daily therapy will help. Our vintage music moves his hands.

"Only Fools Rush In"
"Ain't No Mountain High Enough"
"Leader of the Pack"

He thanks me, squeezes my hand, thanks me again. Follows me with his eyes that no longer crinkle into a smile. He searches for answers while his body sways to the old songs.

"How Deep Is Your Love?"
"Will You Love Me Tomorrow?"
"You Light Up My Life"

Our children come to visit him but don't meet his eyes—touch him tentatively. He can't remember the neighbor's name, but he can mouth lyrics while his feet beat the rhythm.

"The Sound of Silence"
"Bridge Over Troubled Water"
"It's Now or Never"

Not always sure where his body is, in relationship to the chair; he concentrates, but is exhausted and glances at me anxiously. I try to reassure him, take him to therapy and smile. But on the landing strip, he's "Killing Me Softly With His Song."

Hearing Loss

A Sonnet

A rented house atop the rocky cliff
is my abode for weeks beside the sea.
I hang on when the frigid wind is stiff,
because this is a childhood memory.

Today as Pavarotti's tenor soars
from disks another guest has left behind,
I mourn my future lack of ocean's roar,
a coming loss to which I am resigned.

Inhaling saline air my whole life long
while watching spindrift waves lace lava's shore,
praying memory will still hear sea's song.
So, all I want is what I had before.

But I'll use gratitude for my life's guide,
and let my loss go with the ebbing tide.

I Miss You

I fold your plaid flannel shirt,
and the memories it brings.
Tucking it in the Goodwill bag,
it fits with other lonely things.

I'm selling the house
and clothes must be tossed.
Grief reflected in price,
seller will pay closing costs.

We had
        Before
                I lost
                        He loved
All my words are past tense.

He had
        My late
                He was
                        I loved
Moving on is only pretense.

Dementia

Time is chewing
at her loose ropes.
Con   fu
                                        si
                              on
spilling
  like
     coins
from her
         broken bag
of memories.

Her embroidery flourished
stitch by stitch
until
   she lost the thread
and no longer knows me.

I visit
but her eyes
bear the look

of a tide

         gone out.

Precious

Fire-bombed in World War II, Dresden was
a name my father would have known
as he slogged down muddy German roads.
But for me, it was simply the name of
a quilt—Dresden Plate.
The one my mother worked on
for over thirty years,
never seeing the irony.

At ten, I watched her carefully cut
pieces of cloth from my worn-out dress,
the favorite one with black flowers
on red, that added color to my pale face.
She cut blue petals from one of her old
dresses and pink patterned ones
from my younger sister's blouse.

The petals piled up, she arranged them
into a flower, sewed them together
on her treadle machine
and then stacked the quilt flowers.

I wonder if she was disappointed
when her oldest daughter struggled
with sewing. She never said.

Her stack of cloth flowers grew but
wasn't ready to be assembled when I
stood in wedding white.

However, twenty years later, when her
arthritic hands could no longer handle
the needle, she had someone else do
the final quilting and presented me
with my Dresden Plate.

It was too special
to go right on the bed so, it was
carefully folded, wrapped in plastic
and stored in my closet.

There it stayed—precious.

Two years after her death,
I noticed it again. This time,
I spread my bed with memories,
and snuggled down on cold
nights, smelling the love.

Bloodline

The small-blossomed,
blood-red rose
thrusts its gnarled,
thorny stems up,
into my flower bed.

Why is this rose here?
Last year, I dug up
the hybrid-salmon rose
from this very spot,
and left—
nothing.
Or at least I thought
there was nothing.

I stare at the original heritage rose,
the mother rose,
that was grafted and changed
into the more beautiful
composite coral rose
with its larger blossoms,
fewer thorns, longer,
straighter stems.

In the cells
of the roots,
buried just below
the surface,
she was always there.

Looking at my granddaughter's
wide pink mouth,
with that broad upper lip,
I see the grainy
black and white photo
of my great,
great grandmother—
just below the surface.

About the Author

Lorraine Jeffery delights in her closeup view of the Utah mountains after living and working in Texas, New Mexico, Ohio, Georgia, and Oregon. She worked as a public library director for over twenty years, but before she got her master's degree in Library Science, she and her husband raised ten children (eight adopted) and three foster children. She states that the children were more of an education than any university degree. After retirement, she and her husband have visited Great Britain, Ireland, Japan, Thailand, Austria, Canada, Switzerland, and most of the states in the US.

She's won poetry prizes in state and national contests and published over a hundred poems in journals and anthologies, including *Clockhouse, Kindred, Ibbetson Street, Rockhurst Review, Orchard Street Press, The Orchards Poetry Journal, Bacopa Press, Two Hawks, Riverfeet,* and *Naugatuck River Review.* Her stories and essays appear in many publications, including P*ersimmon Tree, Focus on the Family, Elsewhere,* and in Utah anthologies.

Her first book is *When the Universe Brings Us Back* (2022). Her poetry collections with Kelsay Books are *Tethers* (2023) and *Saltwater Soul* (2024).

www.ingramcontent.com/pod-product-compliance
Lightning Source LLC
LaVergne TN
LVHW020651100826
845148LV00012B/2434